THE UNUTTERED LOAD

Sarah Bakshi

BookLeaf Publishing

India | USA | UK

Presentation by *BookLeaf Publishing*

Web: www.bookleafpub.com

E-mail: info@bookleafpub.com

ISBN: 9789363312531

First edition 2024

I would like to thank myself and the people who broke the hell out of me, and also I would like to express my deepest gratitude to my mom, dad, my best friend, my English teacher, pufa pufi, and my nanu, whose support and belief in this project kept me motivated throughout my writing journey.

Special thanks to BookLeaf Publishing for the guidance in the complexities of publishing.

Lastly, I extend my heartfelt appreciation to the readers who will embark on this literary journey. Your interest and engagement with these pages bring meaning to the words I have written.

I WANTED TO SPEAK…….

Bitterness of blossoms

Soaking in the rain
Hoping it will take away the bitterness of pain
Have to give my myself a white rose
And remind myself blossoms dont stay for long,
it slides and goes
Maybe now things are like broken glass
But I know things shall pass
It is sour but true
People vanish in thick air like morning dew.

UNUTTERED LOAD

Late night, I question my existing
I ask myself why is everything twisting
Everything happens for a reason
But what could be the reason of this mystery
Is past really just a history?
Why me? I question myself
Isn't God hearing my bitter cry
Will my word revolve around like this till I die?
Will my world be same under this sky?

GONE TOO SOON

I buried you in my heart, tho u were still alive
As the person I knew was fading in disguise
I have seen you die in your own body and brain
You don't even remember your own name
A part of you died in you
And there I was witnessing the view
Watching you lose all the memories from your
mind
I know love is blind
But mine left a deep scar behind
Where are you, my beloved
Where is the person I loved?

THE LITTLE GIRL

Hiding behind the laughter, the smile
There is a little girl who still tries
She tries her best to hide her loneliness and
sadness from the humankind
People come, tell her lies
They go, she cries
Little girl had a great fall
Now shes hidding in her own made walls
Little girl shy and quite
Doesn't know if she's doing wrong or right
Little girl frightened by the mankind
And tries to be blind
A girl like her can change the world
She can give others a piece of mind

But she hides from the mankind
Save that little girl before she dies
Save her before the time goes and she cries
Save her before she loses her reason to survive.

LAMLET OF THE SOLITARY.

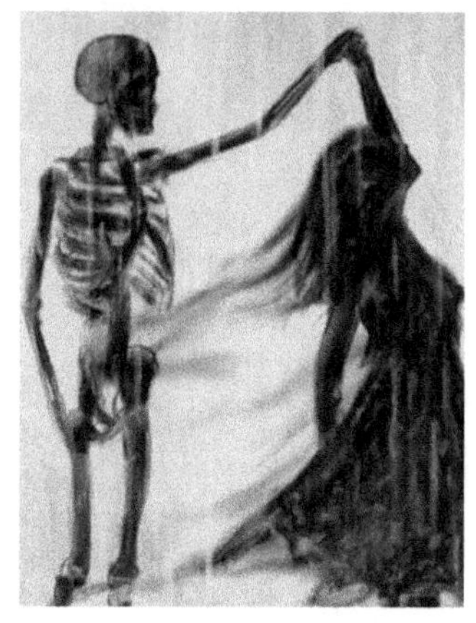

The rain falls softly, like the tears from the sky
In the stillness of night, where shadows weep
and die
There no way out of this beautiful tho desperate
body
In this stunning shell I feel trapped and unsteady
Feels like a black hole Slowly consuming over
my soul
In this dept of night My repentant takes a flight
Feeling lost, deeply trapped in my mind Tears
fall silently, deeply confined

MUMMURS OF THE MIND

Why don't we treat broken souls
Like broken bones?
People hurt themselves
But never say they need help
The broken heart never heals
A heart torn apart, the wounds never seals
Why should people's heart bleed
When help is all they need
There are many words that aren't spoken
They look fine physically but they are
mentally broken
Mental health should be treated as a priority
Mental health our guiding light,

Let's help someone pursue their first healing
flight

WHISPERS OF THE GRAVE: REFLECTION OF LIFES FINAL JOURNEY

Everyone will eventually leave but death shall
never deceive you
It is your faith to go back from where you came
In the darkness and the fame
Death will indeed call your name
eternity and reality are not the same
In the darkest shadows of your name
U will be called again
U shall go to where you came

HURT ME ONCE ONE!

I remember what you said
Probably made me overthink the whole day in
bed
I remember the last time we met
U brought me some tears as presents
I tried ignoring it all
But I wasn't able to ignore your call
After a while my eyes shouted and said we can't
handle it anymore
This was the time my tears started falling
The time was not far where I was willing to take
my life away

The words u said
Were striking in my head
This won't go the pain
This pain is tied in my heart with a restless chain
I'm tired of pretending all these lies
Everytime I laugh its fake
It's simply that I'm hurt
I'm hurt! heart cries silently and unheard
Was it ok to cross the line
U broke me one more time
I wish I could let go
I wish I could start it fresh
It's all done
Memories fade one by one.

FALSE COATING!

Am I a human or a bin?
I can't continue to put on this fake skin
After cleaning people's dirt
Why do I always end up getting hurt?
Why are people so hypocritically dressed
What am I if not dispossessed
Am I that easy to displace?
Not for long, I can continue to make this fake
face

EMBRACING THE ABSENCE.

Tho this distance is new, In my dreams we still meet
Even if we don't speak
Silence echoes, sorrows run deep
I can't forgive u for creating this hollow hole
Tho, you are still in my heart and soul
Despite me, struggling to kick you out of my
never-ending memories lying by my bed
You are still in my head
With every heartbeat, your image remains same
like the love unsaid
Why are u still roaming in my head?
In spite me saying I don't care
I really wish u were here

Yes! We don't speak
But I miss you wiping tears from my cheek
I feel your absence more than your presence
In your absence, these memories are a relentless
essence.

Hearts agony

It's 3 am and again i m crying
I look normal physically
But emotionally I'm dying
Why I m remembering all these lies
I'm fed up from the world, where truth dies
Your beautiful eyes, tho fake still memorize
Through the dark sky, let me fly
Give me back my wing, help me touch the sky
Here darkness overpowers and dreams are
cursed
Love flickers, things get worst
Please Lend me the cup of love and hope
So that I can wipe off my Never ending thirst
Take my cup filled to the brim
With love and hope, your thirst with memories
dim

Since u left.

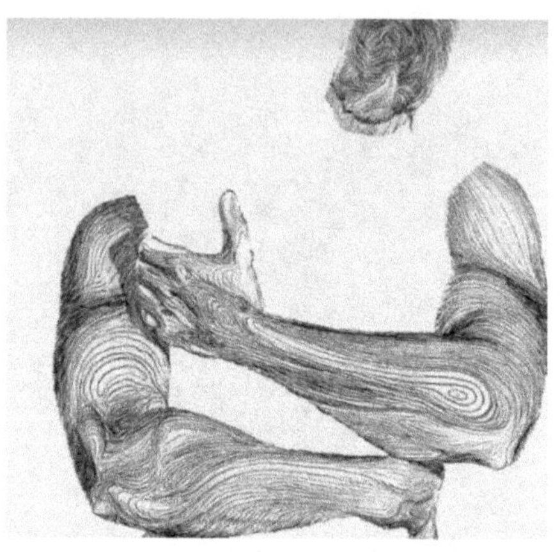

Everyday after u left I have u protected
All the memories that I have collected
Sometimes the weight feels too much to bear
This world seems so unfair
Though the loved ones are gone there neglection
still whispers I'm always here
In the gloomy coners of room where questions
appear
Everyday after u left u broke me more
Leaving unhealed wounds which I still explore
Each day without your presence, shatters me
more
No one was able to hurt me this bad before
Everyday since u left I have been questioning
my ownself

Since u left, living has became my daily quest
I'm really not that strong
Surviving each day feels so challenging and long
Since you left I have been facing everything
alone
This pain was ours, Somehow now I made this
my own.

Questionmark?

Laying in my bed
Questions run in my head
Things I try to forget, tho regret is all I get
A badge of failure which I cannot forget
Revenge taking control over my head
Question echoes, what storm lies ahead
A tag of being a burden like a tear I can't shead
Is life worth hanging on this thread?
I want a break from mistakes I make
Things are getting soo dark
My life is slowing turning into a questionmark

In the darkness of my head Questions expand
their mark
Questions haunting me tearing me apart
Guilt a heavy load I bear
It weights heavy too much to share

WHO AM I?

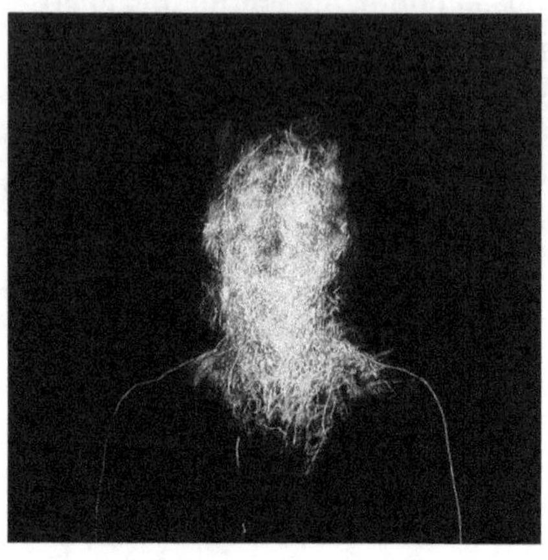

Lost in the darkness of my mind
Searching for myself whom I can't find
Each passing day I discover a stranger in me
Which I'm not willing forward to be
This question echoing within me
Will I ever be able to be free?
Searching for the person I used to know
But who am I now? Help me where should I go?
Fighting for myself in this endless night
I search for a path to regain my light
Each breath a burden, each moment a repentant
flight
Against myself who swallows her own light
Who am I beneath this mask I wear?
What's my true identity under the cover I share?

With every breath sorrows run deep
I seek the truth of who I am, burried under the
secrets I keep
I don't even know myself
Drowning in this sea
I search for my answer, who am I? What makes
me, me,

ANXIETY: THE SILENT PANIC

The feeling which takes me to my past
I wonder how much time is this anxiety is gonna
last
I try my best so that I don't cry
I can't catch my breath tho I try
My heart is beating so fast
I'm cold and shivering on my past
I feel so scared and quite
Don't know if I am doing alright
I feel scared
People are looking at me, I'm not prepared
The worst part is the fact
Now people will think I overreact
Maybe this time I will lose

Maybe death is what I will choose
But in case I survive
This time I won't be found
U won't see me around
I will be hiding in the walls I made
With time my memories will also fade
But if i succeed?
Tears flow freely, like a river of despair
This world isn't understanding its unfair
I gave up on life
A tear falls down my cheek
I'm not brave enough to speak
I took my life with the help of a knife
This was the time I totally gave up on my life

THE DAY I KILLED MYSELF

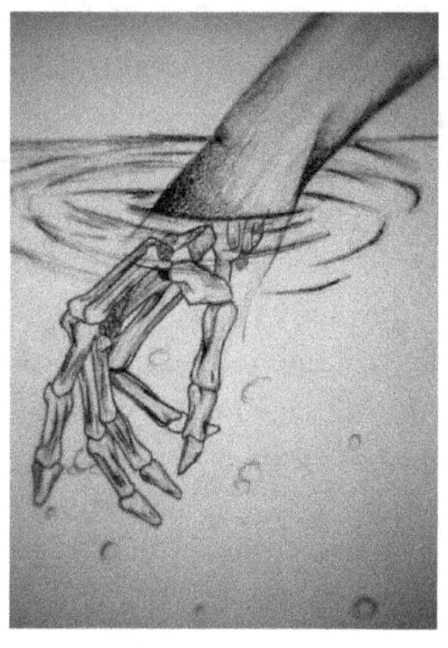

The day after I killed myself was long
The day I chose to end my song
The tears I saw from my parent's eyes
They were in a suprise
Thoughts were running in their mind
Truth is what they declined
My friends were in tears
They were remember me in their prayers
They were lost in the thought of how we spend
our school years
My parents went to my room

It's our fault, They assume
They were staring at the wall
Remembering the baby whom they taught to
crawl
My brother's eyes were red
He wasn't accepting the fact that I was dead
In his gaze, words unsaid
Why did I cut my thread
The day I killed myself was so wrong, they
didn't deserve this pain which was so strong
I tried to undo what I did but it was too late
This time i wasn't able to change my fate

Unspoken wounds

When u need a hug
Cutting works like a drug
When u need help
U can borrow a blade from your shelf
Blood on the floor
Things get too heavy to take any more
Blade by your side
Scar's to hide
Cuts deep in the skin
Wondering what life could have been
Anger, guilt, and pain
Taking control over your brain

It was never an enemy who caused my pain to
ache
The people dear to me caused my heart to break
On my arms, wounds so deep
What happened to me? This time my heart did
weep
Does self-harm reduce my inner pain?
Or leave their marks that remain?
This pain never seems to heal
I am left alone, unsure how ending it will feel.

The night I killed myself

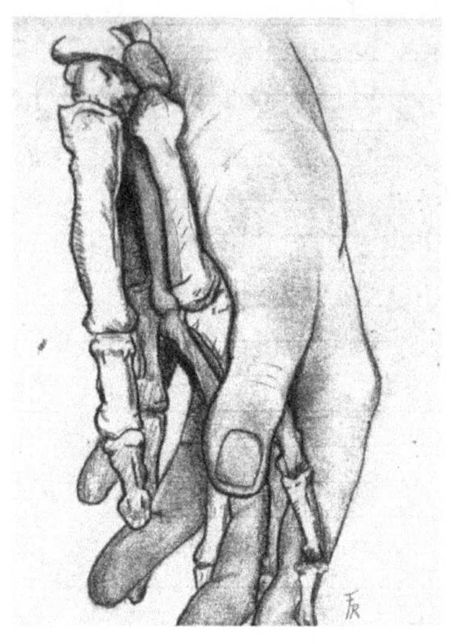

The night was there
Things were gone, which I had to bear
It was so confusing
I felt like I was losing
The ocean of memories came
I had me as a victim and blame
The night came
Took away all the misery and pain
The thoughts I buried
Were feasting on my mind and making me
worried
The night arrived

Took away everything, I couldn't survive
Memories again flooding my heart
Tearing me apart, Tearing me apart
Now my emotions are cold
As I fought demons young and old
The night came
I killed myself in my own burning flame
In this darkness, I fell
I whispered softly, finally a farewell

Hidden emotions

Hidden emotions never die
In future, they might make you cry
Deep down, they r buried
Hiding that you were ever sad, angry, or worried
The more you hide, the emptier you will find
your body and mind
To heal, u must uncover what is left behind

LITTLE HEART OF MINE

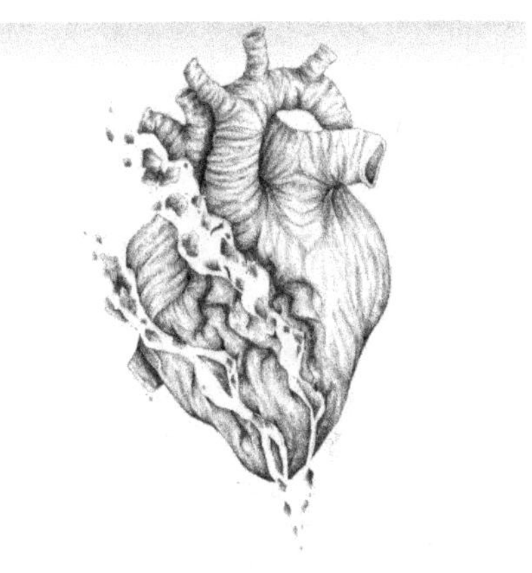

It's getting dark in the little heart of mine
I guess I should work with its design
The small forest in that heart
Slowly falling apart
The butterflies' wings are cut
And the doors to the flowers are shut
The people who lived there are nowhere to be
found
Echoes of people who once lived here now make
no sound
Little heart of mine
Embrace the venom of time

GROWING OLDER

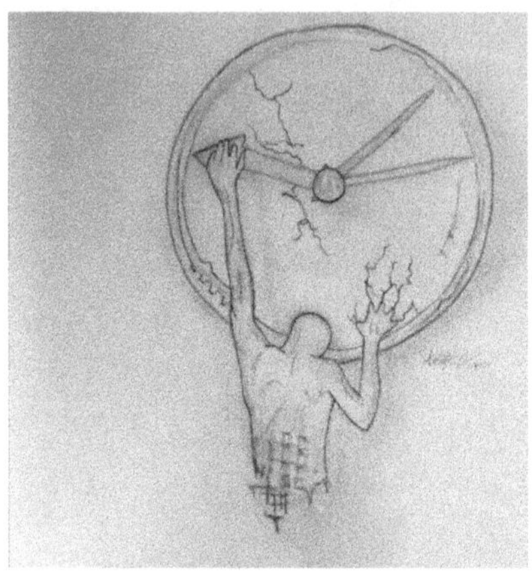

Growing older is a game
Which everyone has to play with a different
name
The older you grow, the more you will fall
You will hear responsibilities making you a call
You would be tired but won't show your
emotions
Life demands strength as its ocean
You would want to be small again
Free from worries and pain
The time you would enjoy small things
Like playing on the swings
Now u miss your childhood days
When life was simpler in many ways

stains of pain

On your favorite shirt I see stains of blood
I can see your eyes full of flood
Who has put this dagger in your heart
Who has ripped u apart?
Who has given u these scars that don't heal
Leaving marks of terror that seems unreal

I won't come back

I won't come back this time
Your memories are criminals will deadly crime
I won't come back
Maybe respect is something u lacked
If u rip my body and see my inner soul
You will see how bad u left me alone
You will see how bad u hurted me creating this
shalllow hole
I'm hurt as I thought u were different from others
U proved me that all humans are produced by
the same mothers
I won't come back again
Reptiles and bugs started eating my body and
brain
They will get a taste of you
Without you I am who?

This time I promise I will leave u untroubled
Carrying the memories of weight which has
doubled
I wonder what we used to be
But this loss is what I can't see
I bid a goodbye with a heavy heart
Knowing that now my life will fall apart

Marks of trauma

She's scared and quite
 Don't know if she's doing alright
She loves staying in the dark
Prefers the solitude in the park
Once she was awesome
A flower of blossom
Things changed her made her cold
Her change was uncontrolled
Things in her head were untold
She was tired of pretending
Her hope was slowly ending
I wanna be dead, she said
On her heart people did a dirty piece of art
She fall apart
The girl is gone
Deep in the sea she drawn
She will lose
Death is what she will choose

Help her before she is dead
She will choose death
Help her before she takes her last breath
A storm going inside her head

Torn thread

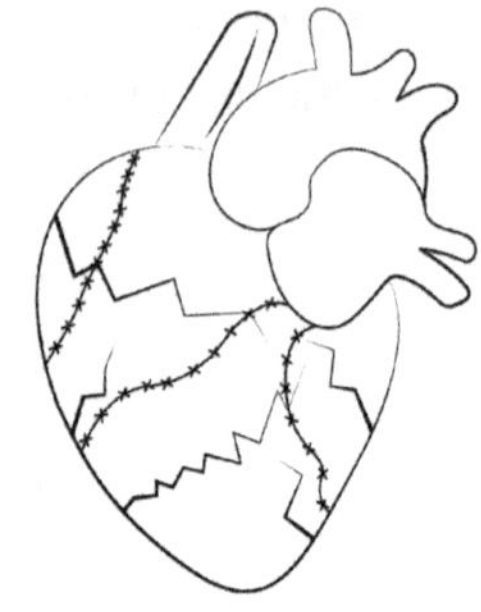

Her vision about life is blurr
Look people what u have made her
once a joyful child
Now she doesn't even remember the last time
she smiled
She is willing to kill herself
But won't ask for help
She is neither alive nor dead
Hanging by a thread
Is it her life or a torn shred

Lost filos

I don't know what to do
Everything holds me back to you
The things we used to do
The happiness I found in you
Moments we shared
The happiness we once paired
I guess being strangers again is the best thing to
do
Dear amica
All the lines have been crossed
On the way our friendship somewhere got lost

Road to death

It is a blessing
It is a curse
Death is the road to a black universe
If you take this road
It isn't far
But it is too complicated to be driven by a car
When try to take your breath
You are on the road of death
Grief is what you will not see
From life you will be free
The road to death can be fun
In order to ride it u may need a gun

If blood haunts u, u can try medicines too
If not once do it twice
Death is entering a paradise

Echoes of deja vu!

I have been here
Where these moments i have to bear
In this endless tho long night where Deja vu! Is
on its height
I have been here
When life starts feeling so ungrateful and not
fair
Is there a place to go if yes where?
Night my enemy tho friend
Guilt and pleasure both it send
Someone to talk but whom
Who is there in this dark room
Maybe me
But do I know who I am or can be
Probably no
Lost in thoughts nowhere to go
Feeling so down can't find a way
This darkeness is now were I stay

Thought to die

Night time it is
No one there is
Darkness is what I see
In the mirror a reflection of me
That reflection is broken and is in tears
But the thing is no one cares
A sudden thought comes in my mind
Which gives me a feeling of peace
Can I really be on ease?
A thought to close my eyes
A thought to end these silent cries
A thought to fly
A thought to spread my wings in the sky
A thought to die,
no more pretending no more lies
Just peace where sorrow dies
Release the burden of years
No more strugle, no more tears

The other part of me

No one knows what's inside of me
I reveal the world what I chose them to see
The smile and happiness everyone sees that is
just a part of me
I allow everyone to see the kindness and
lovingness inside of me but that is just a part of
me
The other half is evil
It is hidden inside a place which is deep
It is filled with loneliness and sadness were fear
rules the seas
A part of me which no one can see
A place I am scared to go
It's all dark and dim
Apart from everything

Elements of solitude

I'm not a human
I'm an ocean where my expectations drowned
Where darkeness wore its mighty crown
I'm not a human
I'm a the heat
Who replayed every gloomy moment on repeat
I'm not human
I'm the moon
Who people leave too soon
I'm not a human
I'm the sun
Shining bright but alone
With no one to call my own
I'm not a human
I'm a star
With scars that never heal
And suffer from memories that I have to deal
I am not a human

I'm a rain
With a smile i wash away all my pain
I'm not a human
I'm the earth
There is no value of me since birth
I'm not a human i m the night
I sleep where shadows weep and fight.

Lost and alone

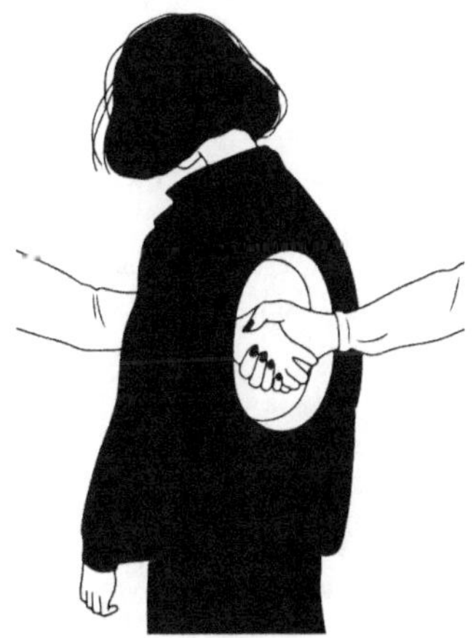

For once I thought I had grown
My struggle seemed to be over thrown
Little did I know
The anxiousness within me will only grow
For once I thought the storm has passed
But little did I know it would last
For once I thought things will be at peace
But then suddenly the wild winds increased
Little did I know
Chaos will soon show
For once I thought I found my way
Through the struggles of night and day
Little did I know hope will turn into despair
Leaving my heart burning with fear
For once i thought the living desire will stay
Little did I knew I will again lost my way

Little did I knew this path would twist
The moments of bliss will soon turn into mist.

New beginning

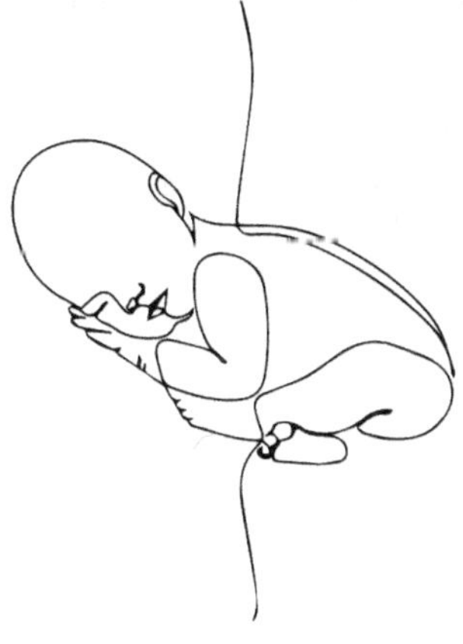

Someone new I met
But your memories I can't forget
He asked me my favorite shade
Things from which I am afraid
He asked me my favorite food
Left me feeling good
Someone new came into my view
Tho thoughts of u still leave me blue
I should see him for what he is
Not based on my past quiz
He is very good
But if u will ever come back to my hearts
neighborhood
He is kind
But thoughts of u coming back continues
playing on my mind

I fear if I get attached to him
Maybe because my heart is filled to the brim
With memories of u its hard to let go
Yet he shows me love I never came to know
He understands my past
My my heart still wonders if he is gonna last.

From the perspective of her diary

She tells all her unhearded words to me
To her darkness I'm the shadow key
She opens me when she is heartbroken
When her thoughts and words are unspoken
She call me her friend
She writes in my pages where she doesn't have to pretend
Sometimes I wish I could speak and tell her how strong she really is
I can just absorb like a stone
I see her crying alone
She tells me all her secrets
She tells me all her regrets
Hi I am her diary, the only one she trusts
Where she lays her naked soul without fear of betrayal or disgust
In my pages her sorrow and joys blend
A loyal secret keeper from beginning to end.

Time a bittersweet experience

And there I stood
Beneath those chair of wood
Where we once used to sit and play
day by day times goes and my hair also turns
grey
Time is like blossoms they slide and go
Leaving a mark of how fast we grow
Aging a bittersweet experience
Learning life lessons, exploring world and
finding sense
Once I questioned what future holds tight
Or used to stay in my past where memories took
flight

But I never stayed in present
Always chasing past or future
Never remembering I will miss this present time
as my tutor
No longer I question what may or might have
been
I cherish now as it is where the present is seen
As time flies it leaves a trace
But every moment in present lived fully adds
lifes grace

MASOCHISM: self injury

the blood pours down my skin
And the tears fall down my chin
I have the blade by my side
When I try to hide
The cuts on my vein
It overcomes all my pain
People will say I died from suicide
But no one knows how hard I tried
It was not a blade or a rope
They had words from which arrows they stroke
When the blade tears my skin
I wonder where my mind has been
The blood gives me peace
It provides me with ease
Long t-shirts will cover my arm
Cover the anger n bruises of self-harm

Only if I knew

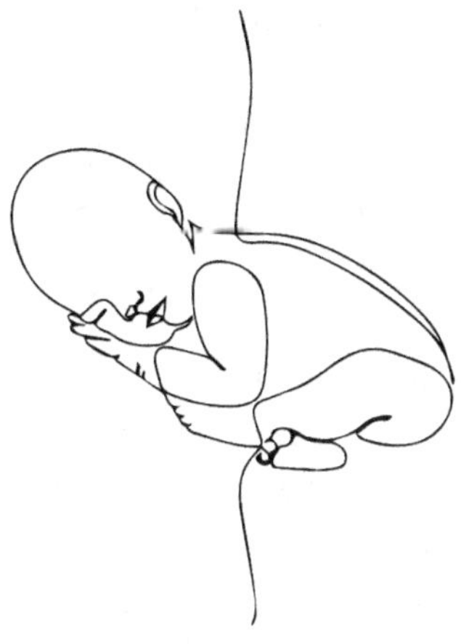

If only I knew, I would never see myself the
same again
If only I knew I would be consumed by my pain
These unspoken words will haunt my mind
In the shadows of what I left behind
Deeply confined to my sorrow
Will there ever be a brighter tomorrow
Searching for someone lost and alone
Only if I knew I have no home
In a void no scope of hope
Were struggles deepen difficult to cope
Is there some light I can borrow
This darkness is leading to sorrow

lost love

The love I once known
Is lost where our bond has flown
The plants of love we once planted died
Just like the tears I cried
Since u slipped away in the night
Even the stars lost their light
Was it so difficult to love me, Dear?
Was my love too much to bear
Why did u leave me in this despair
Memories haunt were u once used to be
The places filled with emptiness now where
once we both used to be
In my heart leaving behind your smile
A memory a beacon of light

BEHIND THE OLD SOUL

57

They call me a old soul who thinks deep
But I am just a young soul,from childhood alone
I weep
They say I am wiser than my years
They just dont know I am a person filled with
emptiness and fears
They say I care like a mothers affection
But they don't know how bad I wanted that
connection
They say u always stay in your solitude zone
How do I tell them I lost my home?
They call me a old soul with wisdom and grace
But they can't see this heartache on my face
I am good in faking, is that the reason why they
claim
I am young soul with a mature brain???

DEATH!

Oh death! Why are you so attractive
Why is your touch so peaceful tho dramatic
Oh death! I m waiting for u to come feat on me
Oh death come set me free
Oh death how much time should I await?
Why are u so late?
Should I come to you or patiently wait
Oh death please open your gate
How much should I wonder around your shore
To live in this world or do I want something
more?
Death if I come to u on my own
Will my death be selfishly known?
Is it selfish to end this fight
Is it selfish to run from the night?
Is peace wrong to ask?
How much time should I continue to pull on this
fake mask?